QUESTIONS
and
ANSWERS

Hundreds of Questions About People, Animals and Places,
With Facts and Surprises for Children on Every Page

BY HORACE ELMO

PICTURES BY TIBOR GERGELY

GOLDEN PRESS   SYDNEY

How Much...

1. How many geese must be plucked to furnish enough feathers for an average-sized pillow?

2. How many languages are spoken throughout the world?

3. How much time does it take to make a good Panama hat?

ANSWERS

1. Eighteen big geese will give three pounds of feathers, enough for a pillow.

2. About 3,000 not including many thousands of dialects.

3. As long as a year, to make the finest Panama hat by hand.

QUESTIONS
and
ANSWERS

CONTENTS

and How Many?

4. How much milk is required to make a pound of butter?

5. How much of the earth's surface is covered by water?

6. How much raw material would be needed to obtain one pound of radium?

7. How many sensations of taste are there?

8. How many parts are there in the average car?

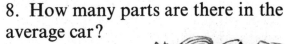

9. How many bubbles will a pound of soap make?

10. How much of Greenland is covered by glaciers?

ANSWERS

4. At least 10 quarts.

5. 71 per cent.

6. No less than 2,680 tons!

7. Only four: sweet, sour, bitter, salty. All other tastes or flavours are combinations of these.

8. About 15,000 different parts.

9. 25,500,000 bubbles.

10. More than five-sevenths of Greenland is buried beneath glaciers that are about 6,000 to 9,000 feet thick.

The Sun

1. How hot is the sun?

2. What would happen if the sun came as close to the earth as does the moon?

3. Is the space between the earth and the sun full of light?

4. How large are sunspots?

ANSWERS

1. According to astronomers, it is 50,000,000 degrees Fahrenheit, at the sun's hottest part. But the earth receives only 1/2,000,000,000th of the total heat radiated by the sun. The rest passes into space.

2. Oceans would turn to steam, and the earth would melt.

3. No. There is perpetual darkness in space. The reflected light of the sun is found only in the atmosphere surrounding the planets and planetoids.

4. Sunspots, which are caused by the escape of gases from the interior of the sun, are vastly larger than the earth. Some are 12,000 times the size of the earth.

and the Moon

5. Is the moon larger than the United States?

6. How do the sun and moon cause tides?

7. Has the moon any light of its own?

8. What are the dark patches that the naked eye can see on the moon?

9. How long does it take light to reach the earth from the sun and the moon?

ANSWERS

5. Yes. It is about four-and-a-half times the size of the United States.

6. By acting like huge magnets pulling the earth toward them. The solid land is not visibly affected, but the water takes a new shape because of the moon's pull.

7. No. It shines only by reflecting the light of the sun.

8. The dark patches are large plains on the moon, which reflect less sunlight than other areas.

9. Moving at the rate of 186,000 miles per second, light reaches the earth from the sun in eight minutes and from the moon in 1.2 seconds.

True or False?

1. No animal eats bees.

2. The needle of a compass always points to the North Pole.

3. Both the Atlantic and Pacific oceans can be seen from one place.

4. The owl is the wisest bird.

5. A pumpkin is a vegetable.

6. Thin people suffer more from the cold than fat people.

ANSWERS

1. *False.* The skunk eats bees, paying little attention to their sting.

2. *False.* The needle points to the magnetic pole, which is over 1,000 miles from the North Pole.

3. *True.* Both oceans can be seen from the top of Mount Irazu, in Costa Rica.

4. *False.* There are many birds more intelligent than the owl.

5. *False.* Botanically speaking, a pumpkin is a berry.

6. *True.* Fat people feel the cold less, because their layers of fat make a good insulation against the cold.

Which Animals Give Us Milk?

YAK

REINDEER

CAMEL

GOAT

HORSE

LLAMA

COW

SHEEP

BUFFALO

ZEBU

ANSWER

All of them! People from various parts of the world drink milk from all of these animals.

Where Do We Get These Words?

HIPPOPOTAMUS

CLOCK

NEWS

HAMBURGER

SUNDAE

ANSWERS

Hippopotamus The Greeks called the hippo "river horse," using the Greek words *hippos,* which means horse, and *potamus,* which means river.

Clock From the Latin word *clocca,* meaning bell. Bells were used to indicate the passing of the hours before clocks were invented.

Hamburger From the city of Hamburg, Germany, where the first hamburgers were made.

News It comes from the word new—not, as people often believe, from the initials which mark the four main directions on weather vanes: North, East, West, South.

Sundae From the fact that it was originally a treat sold on Sundays only. The first sundae was made in Two Rivers, Wisconsin, in 1882.

Game Quiz

Do you know which games of today were played by the children of ancient Greece?

SKIPPING

BALL

MARBLES

DRAUGHTS

JACKS

ANSWER

All of them.

Animal, Vegetable, and Mineral

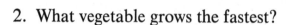

1. What land animal lives the longest?

2. What vegetable grows the fastest?

3. What is the principal crop grown in the United States?

4. What does radium look like?

5. What is the cleanest of all animals?

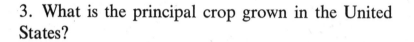

ANSWERS

1. The tortoise. Some have lived for more than 100 years.

2. Asparagus. It grows as much as six inches in a single day.

3. Corn. It covers more acres of ground than all other grains, fruits, nuts, and vegetables combined.

4. It is a whitish substance that looks like common salt or baking powder.

5. The raccoon. Whenever it can get to water it washes its food before eating it.

6. What animal never drinks water?

7. What is the most abundant metal found in the ground?

8. Where are the largest yams grown?

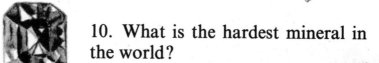

10. What is the hardest mineral in the world?

9. How large can beans grow?

11. What animal is rated next to man in intelligence?

ANSWERS

6. The koala, of Australia. It gets all the moisture it needs from eucalyptus leaves, which are its only food.

7. Aluminium, a silvery-white metal that appears in many compounds, such as clay, mica, bauxite.

8. In the Fiji Islands, South Seas, where yams seven feet long, and weighing 125 pounds, are often grown.

9. Some beans in New Zealand grow to a length of more than seven feet!

10. The diamond. Inferior diamonds called borts and carbonados are used for the points of rock drills and for cutting other diamonds.

11. The chimpanzee, which is considered the cleverest of all animals.

It's for the Birds!

1. How much grain can a sparrow eat in a year?

2. How long do captive parrots live?

3. What bird migrates farthest?

4. Do birds have teeth?

5. Can any bird fly backward?

6. How many kinds of birds are there?

7. Why was the catbird so named?

8. What bird sings loudest?

ANSWERS

1. At least six pounds of grain in one year, and more if he can get it!

2. Captive parrots generally live about 75 years, sometimes 100 years. One parrot in Australia lived 125 years.

3. The Arctic tern is the champion migrator. It nests in the Arctic, and spends the winter in the Antarctic!

4. No birds that can be found in the world today are known to have teeth.

5. Yes. The hummingbird can fly backward as well as forward.

6. There are about 20,000 different kinds of birds in the world. In the United States alone there are about 800 kinds.

7. Because when a catbird is frightened, it makes a sound like the miaow of a cat.

8. The Brazilian bell bird. The voice of this small bird can be heard over a mile away.

9. What bird makes a drumming noise?

10. Can birds whistle with their wings?

11. What bird flies fastest?

12. What bird has no wings or tail?

13. Can birds see better than people?

14. What is the largest flying bird?

15. Do birds have big appetites?

16. Why do many countries protect gulls?

ANSWERS

9. The woodcock. It "drums" by vibrating its feathers.

10. Yes. The hornbill is one bird that can. When it flies, its wings make a shrill whistling sound.

11. The duck hawk holds the speed record for flying—it has been timed at 180 miles an hour.

12. The kiwi. A small, shy bird that feeds at night, the kiwi is found in New Zealand.

13. Yes, much better. Birds have the best eyesight of all living things.

14. The wandering albatross. It has a wingspread of 12 feet.

15. Yes. Some birds eat 50 per cent more than their own weight in 24 hours.

16. Because they are useful scavengers. They eat refuse thrown from ships into the sea, and they eat insects that ruin farmers' crops.

Some Weighty Questions

1. How much does a full-grown lion weigh?

2. Does air have weight?

3. What is the lightest substance in nature?

4. How much does the human heart weigh?

5. How much does a full-grown hippopotamus weigh?

ANSWERS

1. About 500 pounds. When full grown, a lion may reach a height of 3½ feet, and measure 11 feet from the nose to the end of the tail.

2. Yes. To prove it, weigh a football before blowing it up, and again after blowing it up. It will weigh more the second time because of the added weight of air.

3. Hydrogen. A pint of this gas weighs between 1/500th and 1/600th of an ounce.

4. The heart of the average person weighs about 11 ounces. It is 5 inches long, 3½ inches wide, and 2½ inches thick.

5. About 4 tons. The hippo has short legs, and although it may be 12 feet long, it is seldom more than 4½ feet high.

A Whale of a Quiz

1. Is a whale a fish?

2. How much weight does a baby whale gain daily?

3. Do whales spout water?

4. What is whalebone?

5. What is ambergris?

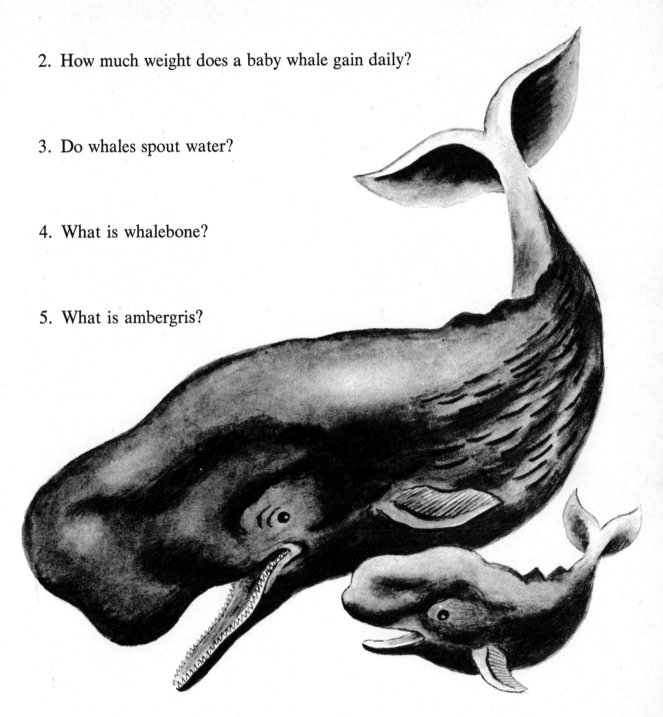

ANSWERS

1. No, a whale is a warm-blooded mammal. Its young are born alive, and are fed on milk from the mother whale.

2. About 200 pounds. Some full-grown whales weigh as much as 100 tons, and are more than 100 feet long.

3. No. They breathe out moist air from their lungs, which condenses into clouds of vapour when it reaches the cool outside air.

4. Whalebone is a horny substance that grows on the roof of the mouth of certain whales. It is not bone at all.

5. It is a greyish, fatty substance given off by the sperm whale. Used in making perfumes, ambergris is five times as valuable as gold.

Up a Tree

1. What tree is cut during moonlight?

3. What tree grows fastest?

2. What tree is the oldest in the world?

4. What trees grow the tallest?

ANSWERS

1. Mahogany is cut by the light of the moon, because at that time the tree has less sap, is sounder, and has richer colour.

3. The bamboo, which is not really a tree at all, but a grass. Bamboo has been known to grow 16 inches in a day.

2. A cypress in Tule, Mexico, which is believed to be from 4,000 to 6,000 years old. It is 125 feet in circumference.

4. The eucalyptus of Australia, and the sequoia, or redwood, of the Pacific Coast of the United States. Both may grow over 300 feet tall, and there are eucalyptus trees over 500 feet tall.

Who?

3. Who first discovered iron in the United States?

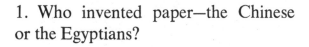

1. Who invented paper—the Chinese or the Egyptians?

2. Who first started the custom of shaving?

4. Who was Geronimo?

ANSWERS

1. The Chinese, in the second century A.D.

3. Sir Walter Raleigh, in 1585. He found iron ore while seeking gold in what is now North Carolina.

2. Alexander the Great. He ordered his soldiers to shave off their beards so that they would not be so easily seized by their enemies in battle.

4. A famous Apache Indian chief who died in 1909. He was the last of the fighting Indian leaders.

What About Insects?

1. Are ladybirds useful or harmful?

2. Do moths eat fabrics?

3. What is the world's largest moth?

4. How fast do a drone fly's wings vibrate in flight?

5. What is the fastest flying insect in the world?

ANSWERS

1. Ladybirds are useful, because they destroy other insects that are harmful to plants.

2. No! They lay their eggs in fabrics, and the larvae feed on fabrics and make holes.

3. The Atlas moth of Asia is more than a foot long, and has a wing-spread of over a foot.

4. About 300 times per second! A hummingbird's wings vibrate 80 times per second.

5. The bot fly. Its average speed is about 50 miles per hour, but on short, darting flights it goes much faster.

6. Can ants swim?

7. Can grasshoppers hear?

8. Do bees obtain most of their nectar from garden flowers?

9. How many bees work to make a pound of honey?

ANSWERS

6. Yes. They can even cross large streams by linking their bodies end to end and forming a chain.

8. No. They get most of their nectar from clover and other wild flowers.

7. Yes. Their ears are at the back of their hind legs. They have very keen hearing.

9. A pound of honey represents the life-work of about 1,000 bees.

Famous People

1. Which king of England could not speak English?

2. Who was the greatest glutton in history?

3. Which American president was oldest when his term ended?

4. Did Magellan sail around the world?

5. What was Christopher Columbus's real name?

6. Which heavyweight champion first fought with boxing gloves?

7. Which American president invented a folding chair?

ANSWERS

1. King George I, who ruled from 1714 to 1727. Born a German prince, he never tried to learn English.

2. The Roman emperor Maximus, who is said to have eaten 50 pounds of meat every day for a number of years.

3. Andrew Jackson. He was 70 years old when his term ended in 1837.

4. Magellan had gone only halfway around the world when he met his death in the Philippines. But 18 members of his crew continued the voyage, and circled the globe.

5. Cristobal Colon. The great explorer never signed his name any other way.

6. John L. Sullivan was the last heavyweight champion to fight with bare knuckles, and the first to wear boxing gloves.

7. Thomas Jefferson. He invented many other things, too, including the dumbwaiter, a plough, a walking stick, a pedometer, a hemp machine, and a kind of printing machine.

Famous Places

1. Which city in the world would take you the longest to cross?

2. Why does Venice have so many canals?

3. Which continent is larger: Europe or South America?

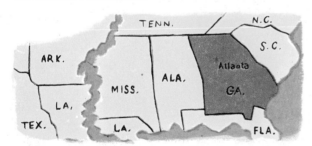

4. What is the largest state east of the Mississippi?

5. Is there a desert in New England, America?

6. Which town has the highest altitude in the world?

7. Is there any city in the world situated on two continents?

ANSWERS

1. Honolulu! Its boundaries extend over 540,000 square miles, most of which is the Pacific Ocean. The town itself is on the island of Oahu, but its administration reaches as far as Midway Island, 1,149 miles west, and Palmyra, 960 miles south.

2. Because the city is built on more than 100 small islands.

3. South America is almost twice the size of Europe, although on the map it looks about the same size.

4. Georgia, which has an area of 58,876 square miles.

5. Yes. It is called the Desert of Maine, and is located near Freeport.

6. Cerro de Pasco, in Peru. This silver-mining town is in the Andes Mountains, about 14,000 feet above sea level.

7. Yes. One half of Istanbul, Turkey, is in Europe; the other half is across the Bosporus Strait, in Asia.

A Capital Quiz

1. Why was the White House painted white?

2. How much time must a Congressman spend in the House or Senate during a session of Congress?

3. How large are the grounds surrounding the White House?

4. Can a woman become president?

5. How long did it take to build the Capitol?

ANSWERS

1. To conceal the fire marks on the walls, after the building was set on fire by the British in 1814.

2. None. There is no law that compels a Congressman to attend any session.

3. About 17 acres.

4. Yes. There is nothing in the Constitution that forbids it.

5. It took over 70 years to complete.

The Great Pyramid of Egypt

1. How many stones were used in it?
2. How much do the stones weigh?
3. How much space does it cover?
4. How long did it take to build?
5. How many men worked on it?
6. How high is it?
7. Who built it?

ANSWERS

1. 2,300,000 stones.

2. An average of 2½ tons each.

3. 13 acres.

4. 20 years.

5. 100,000 men in each relay.

6. 480 feet.

7. Cheops, sometimes called Khufu, a king of ancient Egypt.

27

Of Ships and Sailors

1. What happened to the ship *May-flower*, which brought the Pilgrims to America?

2. Why do sailors wear trousers that are wide at the bottom?

3. Did the famous American warship, *Old Ironsides*, really have iron sides?

4. Would a submarine cruising 60 feet below the surface be affected by a storm at sea?

ANSWERS

1. Its wood was used to build a barn, which still stands at Chalfont St. Giles, England.

2. So that they can roll up their trousers easily when washing decks, or wading in shallow water.

3. No, but its sides were of such strong oak that they deflected English shot during the War of 1812.

4. No, because a storm affects only the surface of the ocean.

Numbers

1. What is the greatest number of loaded coal cars that can be hauled by one engine?

2. How many volumes were in the German encyclopedia, printed between 1813 and 1889?

3. What percentage of the world's supply of grapefruit is raised in the United States?

4. How many people can the Empire State Building, New York, hold?

ANSWERS

1. 183 cars.

3. 97 per cent.

2. 167 volumes.

4. 80,000 people.

Journey into Space

1. How close to the earth is the nearest star?

2. About how many meteors strike the earth's atmosphere every day?

3. Can a star be photographed?

4. When was the moon first contacted by man?

5. Is there life on the planet Mars?

ANSWERS

1. The nearest star is the sun, 93 million miles away. Next is Proxima Centauri, 25 thousand billion miles away.

———

2. About five billion.

———

3. Yes. However, the image of a star caught by a camera is really the light emitted by the star many years before.

4. In 1946, when high-frequency radio waves reached the moon and were echoed back to the earth. The impulses took 2.4 seconds to make the round trip of 477,000 miles.

———

5. Many scientists believe that the temperature and other conditions on Mars may be favourable enough to support some kind of life—probably mosses and lichens.

6. Why is the planet Venus so bright?

7. Are there such things as falling stars and shooting stars?

8. How high does the atmosphere above the earth extend?

9. How does the earth look from the moon?

10. How large is the planet Jupiter?

ANSWERS

6. Because it is surrounded by a cloudy atmosphere which reflects a large proportion of sunlight. And because it is nearer the earth than any other planet.

7. No. They are actually meteors, which are fragments of matter from outer space. They usually vaporise when they near the earth, because of the heat generated by friction.

8. The gaseous envelope surrounding the earth extends about 500 miles. It becomes thinner as the height increases.

9. Very large and bright.

10. The largest planet of our solar system, Jupiter, is over 88,000 miles in diameter—bigger than 1,000 earths!

Where in the World

1. . . . are the hottest places?

2. . . . is it possible to step across the Mississippi River?

3. . . . does the sun look green?

4. . . . does the heaviest rainfall occur?

ANSWERS

1. The world's highest temperature was recorded at Azezia, Tripoli—136.4 degrees Fahrenheit. The highest temperature recorded in the western hemisphere was 134 degrees Fahrenheit, at Death Valley, California.

2. Near Lake Itasca, in Minnesota.

3. In the Antarctic. At sunset, atmospheric conditions cause the sun to appear bright green in colour.

4. In the Amazon Valley, where the average rainfall is 750 inches a year. It receives as much rain in one day as does New York City in 18 months.

What in the World

1. . . . makes an echo?

2. . . . is a prairie dog?

3. . . . is a hurricane?

ANSWERS

1. Sound waves bouncing back after striking a reflecting surface.

2. A little animal belonging to the same family as rats and squirrels. It makes barking noises like a dog.

3. A spiralling wind that blows at more than 75 miles an hour.

The Elephant

1. Does the elephant drink water through its trunk?
2. What kind of meat does the elephant eat?
3. How much water does an elephant drink?
4. How much does an elephant weigh at birth?

ANSWERS

1. No. It would choke if it tried to drink that way. The elephant sucks water into its trunk, then squirts it into its mouth.

3. The average elephant can drink as much as 15 gallons of water at one time.

2. None at all. Elephants are vegetarians.

4. About 400 pounds.

Icebergs

1. What is an iceberg?

2. How do icebergs disappear?

3. How long does it take for an iceberg to melt?

4. How much of an iceberg appears above water?

ANSWERS

1. It is a gigantic mass of ice that has broken off a glacier, or ice-river, of the polar regions.

3. Icebergs last for varying numbers of years, depending on their size and shape. Some are known to have lasted for as long as 225 years.

2. They get carried by currents into warmer seas, and they melt.

4. Only one-ninth of the total mass! The rest is underneath the water.

Is It a Fact?

1. That fleas have wings?

2. That pearls melt in vinegar?

4. That changes in temperature cause tall buildings to lean?

3. That coffee originated in Arabia?

5. That water once started a fire?

6. That Mrs. O'Leary's cow started the great Chicago fire?

ANSWERS

1. No. However, they can hop and jump great distances.

---

2. Yes. A pulverised pearl will dissolve in strong vinegar in about three hours.

---

3. No. Coffee first grew in Abyssinia.

4. Yes. Warm winds, or the sun shining on one side of a building will expand the warm side and cause the top to lean away from the sun. The Washington Monument, in Washington, D.C., sometimes leans one inch off the vertical because of changes in temperature.

5. Yes. A jug of water set off a $5,000 fire in San Francisco. It focused the sun's rays on the dry wall of a house, which burst into flame.

---

6. No. The tale was invented by a reporter who wanted to dramatise his story of the fire. The exact cause remains unknown.

Facts About Food

1. Are there such things as brain foods?

2. Which is more fattening—a pound of butter or a pound of sugar?

3. Are white eggs more nutritious than brown eggs?

4. Which contains the most sugar—peaches, lemons, or watermelons?

5. How much butter is there in buttermilk?

6. Which part of a fowl contains more vitamins—the light meat or the dark meat?

ANSWERS

1. **No.** Any food that nourishes the body nourishes all its parts.

2. **Butter**, which has 3,300 calories per pound. Sugar has 1,800 calories per pound.

3. **No.** White eggs and brown eggs are equally nourishing. The colour of an egg-shell has nothing to do with what is inside it.

4. **Lemons!**

5. **None.** Buttermilk is the liquid which remains when butterfat has been separated from milk.

6. **The dark meat,** which has more vitamin B.

Where and When?

1. When was butter first made?

2. Where do women wear the largest hats in the world?

3. When was paper money first issued?

4. Where did the world's largest hailstones fall?

5. Where were the first oranges grown in America?

6. When was the first "air express" delivery made?

ANSWERS

1. More than 4,000 years ago, when an Arab horseman, riding with a skin of milk, discovered that it had been churned into butter by the galloping of his horse.

2. In Korea. The tent hats worn by Korean women are so huge that they can be used as "wardrobe trunks."

3. More than 1,000 years ago, in China.

4. At Seringapatam, India. Observers in 1870 reported some hailstones the size of elephants!

5. In St. Augustine, Florida. They were planted by the Spaniards about 50 years before the Pilgrims landed.

6. About 900 years years ago, when a caliph of Cairo sent pigeons carrying a supply of cherries to a distant town.

Yes or No?

1. Does a watch tend to gain time at night?

2. Is salt used mainly for the flavouring of food?

3. Is there a plant that can grow through ice?

5. Are camel's-hair brushes made from the hair of camels?

6. Was Indian ink first made in India?

4. Does the fur known as Hudson seal come from the seal?

7. Can a person go without food longer than without sleep?

ANSWERS

1. Yes. The lower temperature at night causes some watches to run faster.

2. No. The most important use for salt is in the manufacturing of chemicals.

3. Yes. The soldanella flower of Switzerland forces its way toward the sun through solid ice.

4. No. It comes from muskrats.

5. No. They are made from the tail hairs of Siberian squirrels.

6. No. It was first made in China, in 1200 B.C.

7. Yes. Human beings have lived for six weeks without food, but no longer than five days without sleep.

Something Fishy

1. How many species of fish are there in the world?

2. What is a sea serpent?

3. How big was the largest shark ever caught?

4. Does a shark grow a new tooth when it loses one?

5. What is the smallest fish eaten as food by people?

ANSWERS

1. There are at least 20,000 species of fish. In no form of life is there a greater variety of shape and colour.

2. The "sea serpent" of myths is probably the oarfish, a long snake-like fish, about 20 feet long and weighing 600 pounds. When it swims, it undulates its whole body into curves, and sometimes appears at the surface of the ocean. It has a red-crested head.

3. Thirty-eight feet long, and 26,600 pounds in weight. It was a whale shark, harpooned off the Florida Keys in 1912.

4. Yes. Sharks can grow an unlimited supply of teeth.

5. The dwarf pygmy goby, only a quarter of an inch long.

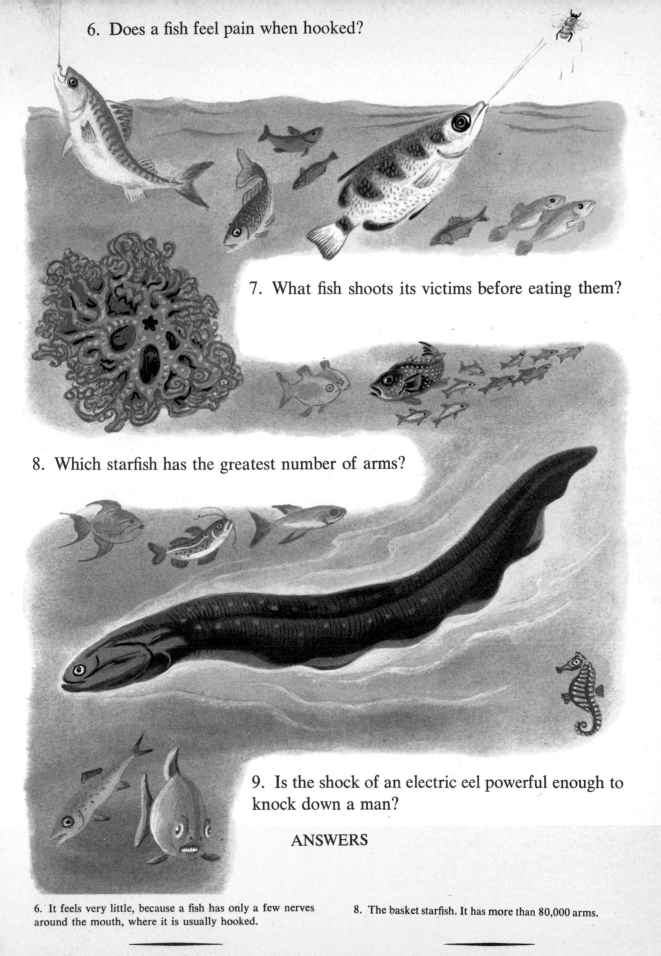

6. Does a fish feel pain when hooked?

7. What fish shoots its victims before eating them?

8. Which starfish has the greatest number of arms?

9. Is the shock of an electric eel powerful enough to knock down a man?

ANSWERS

6. It feels very little, because a fish has only a few nerves around the mouth, where it is usually hooked.

7. The archer fish of the East Indies, which stuns small frogs and insects by shooting them with jets of water.

8. The basket starfish. It has more than 80,000 arms.

9. Yes. The electric eel of South America can generate over 600 volts, and can paralyse even a horse.

Mountains and Volcanoes

1. What is the world's largest active volcano?

2. Do some mountains grow taller with the passing of time?

3. Are there any active volcanoes in the United States?

4. Is it true that some mountain peaks have disappeared?

ANSWERS

1. Mauna Loa, on the island of Hawaii. It is 13,675 feet high, with a crater one-and-a-half miles in diameter.

3. Yes–Mount Lassen, in California.

2. Yes. Mount Izalco, a volcano in El Salvador, was 4,000 feet high in 1770. Today it is about 6,000 feet high, and it is still growing!

4. Yes. The peak of Mount Pele in Martinique vanished during a volcanic eruption in 1902.

Do They or Don't They?

1. Do ascending aeroplanes at an airfield have the right of way over descending planes?

2. Do aeroplane engines make more noise than the propellers?

3. Do American Indian tribes speak more than 100 different languages?

4. Do monkeys shed tears?

5. Do some bananas grow as long as two-and-a-half feet?

6. Do cows have stronger horns than bulls?

7. Do the phases of the moon affect crops?

ANSWERS

1. They don't.

2. They don't.

3. They do.

4. They do.

5. They do.

6. They do.

7. They don't.

Gold and Precious Stones

1. What was the largest gold nugget ever found?

2. What is the most valuable gem?

3. What colour is the famous Hope diamond?

4. Why was the carat chosen as the measure for weighing gold?

5. Where do most of the world's diamonds come from?

6. Can diamonds wear out?

 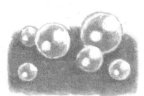   

SAPPHIRE   PEARL   RUBY   DIAMOND   EMERALD

ANSWERS

1. The "Welcome Stranger" nugget, which weighed 2,520 ounces.

2. The Oriental ruby, found chiefly in Burma and Siam. It is a corundum of great hardness, and has many times the value of a diamond of the same size.

3. Very dark blue, almost black.

4. The word "carat" comes from the Arabic *qirat*, which means "pod of the coral tree." The dried seeds of this tree were used to weigh gold because they never vary in weight.

5. From the diamond mines of Kimberley, South Africa, which produce about 98 per cent of the world's output.

6. Yes. Diamonds used in fine-glass engraving plants are worn out by use in six to eight weeks.

A Visit to the Zoo

1. Which is the smallest monkey?

2. Do animals get toothache?

3. How much does a newborn black bear weigh?

4. What animal makes the loudest noise when bellowing?

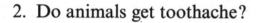

5. Which is the busiest eater in the animal kingdom?

6. Do polar bears in zoos suffer from heat during the summer?

ANSWERS

1. The six-inch pygmy marmoset, of Brazil. It weighs about half a pound, and can sit comfortably in a spoon!

2. Yes, though not as frequently as human beings. Most veterinary surgeons have to be trained in animal dentistry.

3. Less than half a pound! When full grown, however, a black bear weighs a bulky 300 pounds or more.

4. The lion. It is estimated that its roar can sometimes be heard ten miles away. Next loudest are the bull, elk, sea lion, and wolf.

5. The short-tailed shrew, which feeds almost continuously. It consumes its own weight in food every three hours.

6. No. When they are brought to temperate climates they quickly lose the thick layers of fat which keep them warm in their arctic homes.

Strange Animals

1. What little rodent can run as fast as a horse?

3. What animal spends most of its life upside down?

2. What American mammal has a pouch like a kangaroo's?

4. What animal lays eggs like a bird, suckles its young, burrows like a rodent, and has a ducklike bill and feet?

ANSWERS

1. The jerboa. This little creature is sometimes as small as a mouse, but it has very long, strong legs. Jerboas are found in many dry parts of Africa, Asia and Europe.

3. The sloth, which hangs from tree branches with its hook-like claws, and seldom moves if it can help it.

2. The opossum. A mother opossum carries as many as fifteen babies in her pouch until they are quite grown up.

4. The duckbill platypus, found only in Australia and the Island of Tasmania.

The Spider's Web

1. How strong is a spider's web?

2. If a pound of spider web were unrolled, how long would it be?

3. Is there a commercial use for spider web?

ANSWERS

1. For its weight, a spider's web is estimated to be stronger than steel.

2. Long enough to encircle the earth at the equator.

3. Yes. Strands of web are used for cross-lines on range finders, microscopes, and other instruments.

Which State?

1. In which American state did a meteor cause a one-mile-wide crater?

2. Which state has over 11,000 lakes?

3. Which state has 99 lakes named Long?

4. Which is the only state that was an independent republic recognized by the United States before it joined the Union?

5. Which state has something alive that is 4,500 years old?

ANSWERS

1. Arizona. Meteor Crater on U.S. 66 was made by a prehistoric meteor.

2. Michigan

3. Minnesota

4. Texas

5. California. A stand of bristlecone pine in the Inyo National Forest is estimated to be 4,500 years old.

Geographical Giants

1. What is the largest desert in the world?

2. What is the deepest lake in the world?

3. Where are the largest forests in the world?

4. What is the largest reef?

5. What is the highest waterfall in the world?

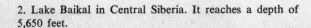

ANSWERS

1. The Sahara in North Africa. It covers 3½ million square miles.

2. Lake Baikal in Central Siberia. It reaches a depth of 5,650 feet.

3. In the northern U.S.S.R. The total wooded area is 2,275,000,000 acres.

4. The Great Barrier Reef off Queensland, North East Australia. It is 1,260 miles long.

5. Angel Falls, Venezuela. It has a total drop of 3,312 feet.

Music and Art

1. What famous composer began to write music at the age of 5?

3. What great composer wrote over 500 pieces of music?

4. What famous man became a musician against his father's wishes?

5. What composer earned money as a boy by playing piano in taverns?

2. What composer wrote some of his greatest music after becoming deaf?

ANSWERS

1. Wolfgang Mozart.

2. Ludwig van Beethoven.

3. Franz Haydn.

4. Johann Strauss.

5. Johannes Brahms.

6. How long did it take Michelangelo to complete the ceiling of the Sistine Chapel?

7. What is the actual name of the painting we call "Whistler's Mother?"

8. What artist began to paint at the age of 76?

9. What famous painter was also a musician, engineer, architect, and scientist?

ANSWERS

6. 4 years. Michelangelo painted scenes depicting Bible stories that covered the ceiling.

7. Arrangement in Grey and Black.

8. Anna Mary Robertson (Grandma) Moses.

9. Leonardo da Vinci.

Of all Things

6. Is there a fish that can travel on land as well as on water?

1. If a crab loses a claw, can it grow a new one?

2. How long a line can be drawn with an ordinary lead pencil?

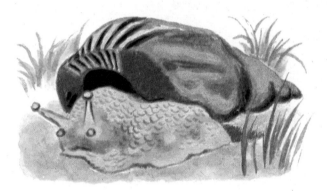

3. Can a cat see better in the dark than during the daytime?

7. How large is the giant land snail of Africa?

4. Is chop suey popular in China?

5. Does hair grow faster in certain seasons?

8. How much of the total atomic energy of its materials does the exploding atomic bomb release?

ANSWERS

1. Yes.

2. A continuous line 38 miles long.

3. No, a cat sees better during the day. However, when there is little light a cat can see better than a person, because its pupils expand more, and let in more light.

4. No such dish is known in China! Chop suey is a 20th-century dish, invented in San Francisco.

5. Yes. It grows faster in summer than in winter, and faster by day than by night.

6. Yes. The fish known as the mudskipper can walk on land and even climb trees.

7. It is six to nine inches long, and as big around as a large orange.

8. Only 1/1,000th of the total energy sealed within the atom.

9. What is the oldest city in the western hemisphere?

10. Where and when was the first cheese made?

11. What body of water contains the most minerals?

12. What is the most dangerous of all small fish?

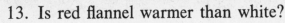

13. Is red flannel warmer than white?

14. How long does a date palm bear fruit?

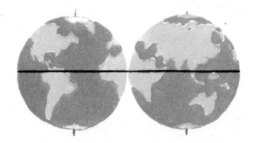

15. Why is the equator called by that name?

16. How was rubber first used?

ANSWERS

9. It is thought to be Mexico City, which was founded in 1325.

10. In Egypt, over 3,000 years ago.

11. The Dead Sea, which is about 25 per cent solid matter—mostly salt. It is eight times more salty than ocean water.

12. The piranha, a South American freshwater fish. Only about ten-and-a-half inches long, this bloodthirsty fish has probably taken more human lives than the deadliest shark.

13. No. Red flannel and white flannel of the same grade and weight are equally warm. Red just *looks* warmer!

14. From two to three centuries.

15. Because it is equally distant from the North and South poles.

16. The Indians of Central America used it to make rubber balls for games!

Getting Around

1. Who were the greatest road builders of ancient times?

2. What was the Red Flag Act?

ANSWERS

1. The Romans. At one time, the Roman system of roads encompassed 180,000 miles.

2. The Red Flag Act was passed in 1836 in England. This law required that a boy riding a horse, and carrying a red flag during the day and a lantern at night, had to ride before every steam carriage.

3. How long did the first engine-powered aeroplane flight last?

4. What is the largest liner afloat?

ANSWERS

3. 12 seconds. It was made by Orville Wright on Dec. 17, 1903 at Kitty Hawk, North Carolina.

4. The *Queen Elizabeth*, former British passenger liner, is 1,031 feet long, 118 feet wide, and has a tonnage of 83,673.

The Human Body

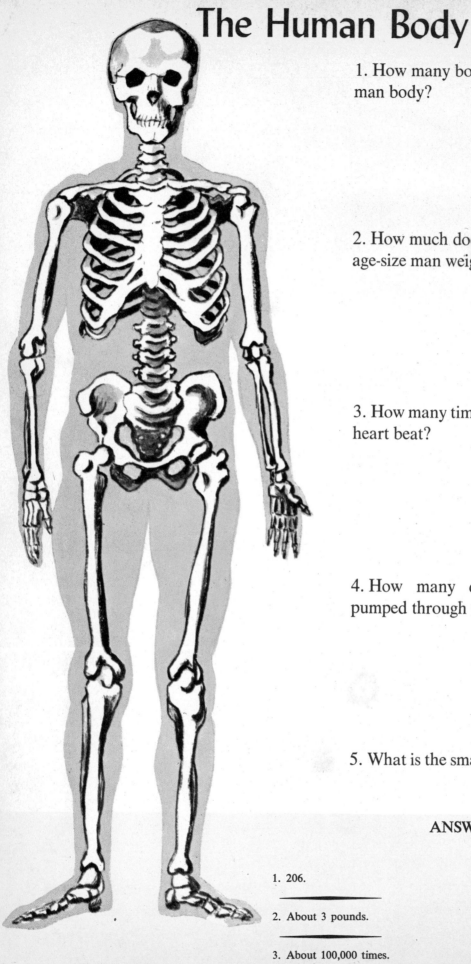

1. How many bones are there in the human body?

2. How much does the brain of an average-size man weigh?

3. How many times a day does an adult's heart beat?

4. How many quarts of blood are pumped through the body each day?

5. What is the smallest unit of life?

ANSWERS

1. 206.

2. About 3 pounds.

3. About 100,000 times.

4. 13,000 quarts.

5. The cell.

How Do They Grow?

Which of the following grow on trees?

WALNUT

OLIVE

PUSSY WILLOW

APPLE

DATE

COCONUT

MAGNOLIA

ANSWER

They all do.

Name the Young

What are the young of each of these animals called?

COW

HIPPOPOTAMUS

MOOSE

ELEPHANT

RHINOCEROS

WHALE

ANSWER

The young of all these animals are called calves.

It's a Dog's Life!

2. Is there a dog that cannot bark?

1. Which shepherd dog herds runaway sheep by jumping on their backs?

3. Is there a dog with a black tongue?

4. Which do you think is the largest of these dogs: Great Dane; Doberman pinscher; Saint Bernard; Irish wolfhound?

ANSWERS

1. The puli, first known in Hungary many years ago. The sheep soon gets tired of running with the dog on its back, and allows itself to be led back to the flock.

3. Yes. The chow-chow has a black tongue. It is also distinguished by its straight back legs, and paws that are rather like a cat's.

2. Yes! the basenji can make only sharp yodelling cries, quite unlike a dog's bark.

4. The Irish wolfhound. It stands as high as three feet at the shoulder.

Snakes

1. Is the boa constrictor poisonous?

2. Are there such things as flying snakes?

3. Can the direct heat of the sun kill a rattlesnake?

4. Do some snakes have legs?

5. What is the largest snake in the world?

6. How do snakes hear?

ANSWERS

1. No. It kills its victims by crushing them in its coils.

2. Some snakes in Java and Malaya can flatten themselves out like ribbons, and sail from tree to tree. They are called "flying" snakes.

3. Yes. The snake cannot stand heat above about 115 degrees Fahrenheit.

4. Yes! Many of the larger snakes have small legs under the skin near the tail.

5. The anaconda, of the Amazon region of South America. It is over 25 feet long, and more than a foot thick.

6. Snakes have no ear openings. Their entire body picks up vibrations from the ground.

Frogs

1. Are there such things as flying frogs?

2. Is there a frog as large as a dog?

3. When frogs hibernate, do they stop breathing?

4. How small is the world's smallest frog?

ANSWERS

1. Yes. The flying frog of Asia can use its webbed feet like a parachute as it sails from tree to tree.

2. Yes. The giant frog of Africa. It is two-and-a-half feet long, and weighs more than 14 pounds.

3. They stop breathing as they normally do, and instead take in air through their skin.

4. The tropical frog of Central Africa is no bigger than a housefly.

61